This Book Belongs To:

Let's Play I Spy

1. Examine each page closely to spot the Valentine's Day themed items listed. Can you find them all?

2. Once you've spotted an item, tick it off or circle it in the list provided nearby.

3. Use your imagination to color the beautiful illustrations after you've completed your spying mission.

4. Share this exciting experience with friends and family, inviting them to join in the Valentine's Day fun!

I Spy with my little eye
Something beginning with...

Arrow

I Spy with my little eye
Something beginning with...

Bow

I Spy with my little eye
Something beginning with...

Cats

I Spy with my little eye
Something beginning with...

Dove

I Spy with my little eye
Something beginning with...

Envelope

I Spy with my little eye
Something beginning with...

F

Fox

I Spy with my little eye
Something beginning with...

Gnomes

I Spy with my little eye
Something beginning with...

I Spy with my little eye

Something beginning with...

Heart

I Spy with my little eye
Something beginning with...

Ice cream

ice cream

I Spy with my little eye
Something beginning with...

Jar

Jar

I Spy with my little eye
Something beginning with...

Key

I Spy with my little eye
Something beginning with...

I spy with my little eye...

Something beginning with...

Lovebirds

I Spy with my little eye
Something beginning with...

Monkey

I Spy with my little eye
Something beginning with...

Nest

I Spy with my little eye
Something beginning with...

Owl

Owl

I Spy with my little eye
Something beginning with...

Padlock

I Spy with my little eye
Something beginning with...

Queen

I Spy with my little eye
Something beginning with...

Rabbits

I Spy with my little eye
Something beginning with...

Sunglasses

I Spy with my little eye
Something beginning with...

I Spy with my little eye

Something beginning with...

Teddy bear

I Spy with my little eye
Something beginning with...

Umbrella

I Spy with my little eye
Something beginning with...

Vulture

I Spy with my little eye
Something beginning with...

Worm

I Spy with my little eye
Something beginning with...

Xylophone

I Spy with my little eye
Something beginning with...

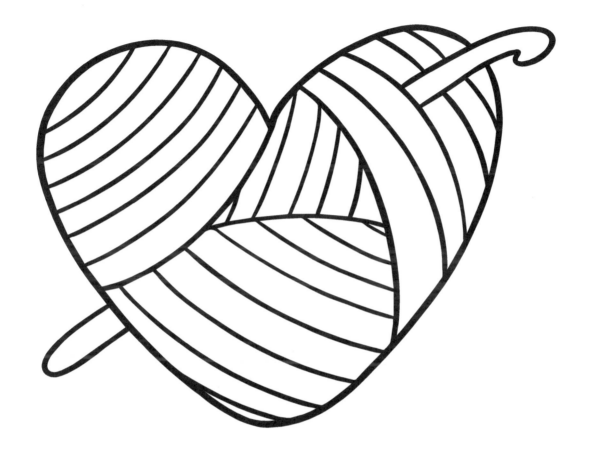

Yarn

I Spy with my little eye
Something beginning with...

Zebra

Made in United States
Troutdale, OR
02/11/2024

17581175R00060